KU-165-765

CONTENTS

YOU'RE *one of a kind,*

AND YOUR ACCESSORIES SHOULD BE TOO.

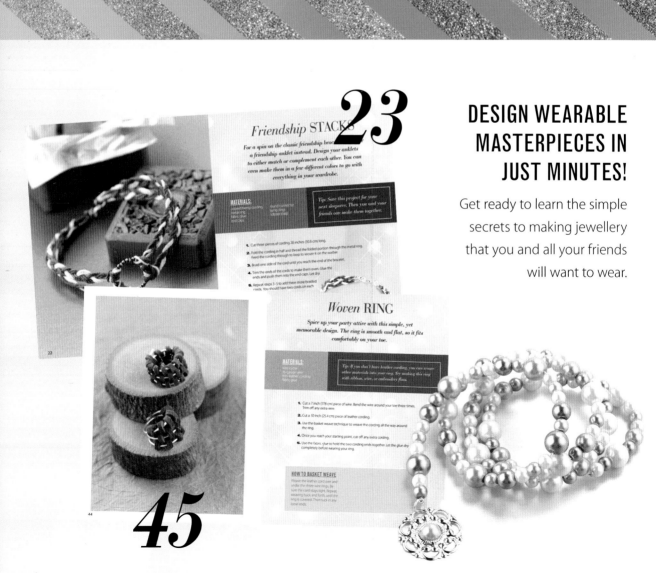

23

45

DESIGN WEARABLE MASTERPIECES IN JUST MINUTES!

Get ready to learn the simple secrets to making jewellery that you and all your friends will want to wear.

Use this book as a springboard to create even more personalized ideas; just embellish the jewellery to reflect your own style. As you create, remember that anklets can play double duty as bracelets, and bracelets as anklets. Likewise, the look of a ring is easily switched up by wearing it on your toe. You can even size up and turn rings into bracelets or necklaces! Jewellery is an art, and there is no right or wrong way to create. Get ready to express your personal style as you dive into this book.

Denim DELIGHT

Do you have an old pair of jeans with grass stains and ripped holes? Or perhaps you have outgrown a comfy fleece or favourite T-shirt. Think twice before you take them to a charity shop. Instead, make a stylish bracelet in minutes.

MATERIALS:

scissors
old jeans, fleece
    or T-shirt
thread
fabric glue

end caps
chain
jump rings
lobster clasp
round-nosed pliers

1. Cut fabric into three pieces, each 25.4 centimetres (10 inches) long by 2.5 centimetres (1 inch) wide.

2. Secure the pieces together by wrapping one end with a 25.4-centimetre piece of thread. Wrap the thread around the fabric ends 20 times, and then knot the thread to hold it in place.

3. Braid the fabric pieces, leaving a 2.5-centimetre tail.

4. Repeat step 2 at the other end of the braid.

5. After both ends are tied off with thread, use the scissors to trim the extra fabric off.

6. Dab some fabric glue in an end cap. Insert one end of the braid into the cap. Repeat on the other end. Let dry.

7. Wrap a chain around the length of the bracelet. Use jump rings to connect the ends of the chain to the end caps.

8. Attach the lobster clasp to the end caps using round-nosed pliers.

Tip: The wider you cut the fabric, the thicker the bracelet will be. Thinner fabric will make for a smaller, daintier bracelet.

MATERIALS:
20-gauge wire
wire cutter
round-nosed pliers
small beads
eye pins
large charm (optional)

Open-ended WIRE WRAP

A wire wrap is the perfect statement piece that's casual enough for school. Get fancy with pearls and crystals, or keep it casual with glass and metal beads.

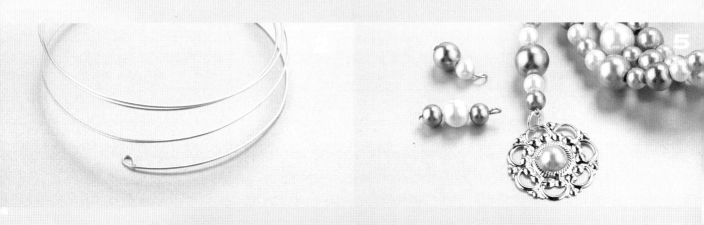

1. Wrap the wire around your wrist 3 to 5 times, and cut the end.

2. Use the pliers to bend one end of the wire into a tiny loop to stop the beads from falling off. The loop also creates a place to connect charms.

3. Thread beads onto the wire until covered.

4. Bend another tiny loop on the other end to prevent the beads from falling off.

5. Create charms by threading one to three beads onto an eye pin. To finish the charm, bend a loop with the end of the eye pin wire and wrap the tail around itself. If the tail is too long, trim it with the wire cutter.

6. Attach charms to both loop ends of the bracelet. You can also add the large charm, if desired.

Tip: Maintain a minimalist look with beads in all one colour or style. Or go bold with a fun pattern of brightly coloured beads.

MATERIALS:

scissors
2.5-centimetre-
  wide ribbon

buttons
needle and thread
  (optional)

Button NECKLACE

If you enjoy sewing in your free time, this bracelet is for you! Put your crafty talents to work by sewing colourful buttons onto ribbon to make a uniquely styled bracelet.

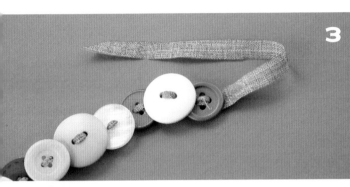

3

Tips: Cover buttons with fabric or scrapbook paper and decoupage glue. Layer small buttons over larger buttons, or decorate with glitter.

1. Cut the ribbon to your desired necklace length.

2. Lay the buttons alongside the ribbon in the desired pattern.

3. Thread the ribbon through the buttons. (If the button holes are too small, use a needle and thread to sew the buttons to the ribbon.)

4. Adjust the buttons so they are centred on the ribbon. Then knot the ends of the ribbon to keep the buttons in place.

5. Cut two 10.2-centimetre- (4-inch-) long pieces of ribbon. Tie one in a bow around one of the knots you tied in step 4. Repeat on the other side of the necklace.

MATERIALS:

small round beads
eye pins
round-nosed pliers
16-gauge wire

wire cutter
small square jump rings
small round jump rings

Caged bead
CHARM BRACELET

Get up close and personal with caged beads. Create your own charms using fancy caging techniques, beads and tiny trinkets.

FOR STYLE A:

1. Thread three beads onto the eye pin.

2. Use the round-nosed pliers to bend a closed loop in the top of your eye pin, wrapping the extra wire around itself.

3. Coil wire around the beads. Wrap one end around the eye pin loop. Twist the other end of the wire to create a loop at the bottom of the beads.

FOR STYLE B:

1. Cut a 5-centimetre (2-inch) piece of wire. Shape the top part in a tight coil, and then do the same with the bottom piece but in the opposite direction to create an 'S' shape with the wire.

2. Slip the bead or trinket in the middle and pull the coil over it to enclose it. Create a loop with the wire on one end to attach to a jump ring. Cut off any excess wire.

3. Use jump rings like bracelet links, attaching the charms to each other.

Tip: For a different look, change up the finish of the wire. Try gold, antiqued or coloured metal.

MATERIALS:

2-mm leather cord
button

seed beads
small jump rings

Stylish seed BEADS

Sometimes shop-bought presents just won't do for the special person in your life. Instead, surprise them with this long-lasting leather bracelet. It's a gift your friend can treasure forever.

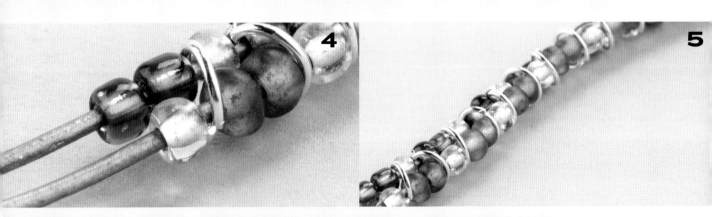

1. Cut a piece of leather cord 38 centimetres (15 inches) long.

2. Thread the button onto the cord and tie a knot to keep it at the centre of the cord.

3. Place two seed beads on one half of the cord and one seed bead on the other half.

4. Thread two jump rings over both pieces of cord until they hit the bottom of the beads. Place two seed beads on the piece with one bead, and one seed bead on the cord with two beads.

5. Thread two more jump rings over the cord. Repeat this pattern until most of the cord has been covered.

6. Knot the two pieces of cord together. Leave 1.3 centimetres (½ inch) space and tie a second knot to create a hook for the button clasp. Trim off any extra cord.

Tip: Replace the leather cord with embroidery floss or wire. Make a few bracelets and wear them stacked together!

Triple strand DELIGHT

Accessorizing accents in groups of threes or fives draws the eye and shows off your style. A simple way to achieve this look is with the Triple strand delight. Bead three bracelets in three different styles, then connect them onto one clasp to create a 3-in-1 beauty!

MATERIALS:

embroidery floss
scissors
beads in three styles
jump rings

round-nosed pliers
crimp end caps
  with loops
clasp

Tip: Use similarly coloured beads and floss to create a uniform look, or get colourful by using different coloured beads and floss for each strand.

1. Wrap embroidery floss around your wrist. Add 2.5 centimetres (1 inch) and cut. Repeat this step two more times.

2. Tie the three pieces of embroidery floss together at one end, leaving a 1.3- centimetre (½-inch) tail.

3. Decorate one strand with all the beads touching each other. Knot the end to keep beads in place.

4. Bead the next strand with the second type of bead. Add a knot between each bead, then make a final knot at the end.

5. Bead the last strand with a third type of bead. Spread out your knots to create a strand with even fewer beads. Make a final knot at the end. Then tie the ends of all three strands together, leaving a 1.3-centimetre (½-inch) tail.

6. Use the pliers to crimp an end cap at both ends of the bracelet.

7. Connect the clasp to one end cap using jump rings.

Wire and bead BANGLE

Wire creates a modern look, but adding curls and twists softens the vibe. Try stacking a few colour-coordinated bangles for added dimension.

MATERIALS:

wire cutter
24-gauge wire
round-nosed pliers
beads
14-gauge wire

Tip: Use similar steps to make matching rings, earrings and necklaces.

1. Cut the 24-gauge wire to the desired bracelet length (once around your wrist). Add an extra 0.6 centimetres (¼ inch) for the looped ends.

2. Use the pliers to bend one end into a small loop.

3. Thread beads onto the bracelet until all but the last two centimetres are decorated. Bend the other end of the wire into a loop to keep the beads from falling off.

4. Tightly wrap the 14-gauge wire around one end of the bracelet several times until you reach the first bead. Cover the end of the thin wire as you wrap.

5. Wrap the wire between and around the beads until you reach the other end of the bracelet. Cut the wire, then tuck the end under the wraps.

Lacy WRISTLET

This bracelet is elegant and whimsical. Practise your sewing skills as you create this beauty. Plan to use lace and beads all in the same colour, or get imaginative mixing different shades.

MATERIALS:

wide, heavy lace
scissors
needle
thread

pearl and crystal beads
ribbon
fabric glue

Tip: Use pearl and crystal beads to make this elegant bracelet. For an everyday look, use glass or metal beads.

1. Measure and cut the lace to fit around your wrist.

2. Start at one end of the lace and begin sewing the beads along the pattern of the lace. Continue until the lace is covered with the desired number of beads.

3. Cut two 12.7-centimetre (5-inch) pieces of ribbon. Use the needle and thread to sew one ribbon to one end of the bracelet. Repeat on the other side with the second ribbon.

4. Secure the bracelet onto your wrist using the ribbon to tie a bow.

Friendship STACKS

For a spin on the classic friendship bracelet, consider a friendship anklet instead. Design your anklets to either match or complement each other. You can even make them in a few different colours to go with everything in your wardrobe.

MATERIALS:

coloured hemp cord
metal ring
fabric glue

end caps
jump rings
lobster clasp

Tip: Save this project for your next sleepover. Then you and your friends can make them together.

1. Cut three pieces of cord 50.8 centimetres (20 inches) long.

2. Fold the cord in half and thread the folded portion through the metal ring. Feed the cord through the loop to secure it on the ring.

3. Braid one side of the cord until you reach the end of the bracelet.

4. Trim the ends of the cords to make them even. Glue the ends and push them into the end caps. Let dry.

5. Repeat steps 1–4 to add three more braided cords. You should have two cords on each side of the metal ring.

6. Use jump rings to attach clasps to the end caps.

Feathers and RIBBON

Channel your inner hippie with this whimsical look. Mixed textures add depth and complexity to any jewellery. Pick your favourite combinations of coloured feathers and ribbon to make this unique trendsetter.

MATERIALS:

0.6-cm- (¼-inch-) wide ribbon
fabric glue
7 small feathers, about 5 cm (2 inches) long

2.5-cm (1-inch) fringe ribbon (optional)
ribbon clamp
round-nosed pliers
jump rings
clasp

Tip: If you can't find small feathers, simply cut longer feathers into 5-centimetre pieces. You can also make your own faux feathers using felt, suede or other heavier fabrics. Use a stencil or create your own freehand style.

1. Cut two pieces of ribbon to fit around your ankle.

2. Lay one piece of ribbon flat. Place dots of glue along the ribbon, each about 1.3 centimetres (½ inch) apart.

3. Place the ends of the small feathers or the fringe ribbon on the glue.

4. Squeeze a thin stripe of glue over the feathers. Press the second piece of ribbon on top of the first.

5. Attach a clamp to both ends of the ribbon. Secure with glue.

6. Use jump rings to attach the clasp.

MATERIALS:
round-nosed pliers
jump rings
seed beads
lobster or toggle clasp

Jump ring CHAIN

Did you ever make paper chain decorations when you were younger? Here's the bejewelled version. Instead of paper strips, use shiny metal rings and sparkling beads to make an ankle bracelet.

Tip: Jump rings are small metal rings used for crafting. They are sold in sizes between 2 mm and 20 mm and come in many different metals and finishes. Try making your own jump rings. Coil 16-gauge wire around a pen or pencil four or five times. Remove the coil and use a wire cutter to cut the rings.

1. Use the pliers to open a jump ring. Thread on two beads.

2. Close the jump ring to hold the beads in place.

3. Open the next jump ring and link it with the first jump ring. Close it without adding any seed beads.

4. Open another jump ring and thread on two beads. Hook it into the previous jump ring and squeeze it closed. Follow this with an empty jump ring.

5. Continue the pattern until you have reached the desired length.

6. Attach the clasp to the jump rings at both ends of your anklet.

Thumbprint
CHARMER

This anklet has you bringing the crafts to the kitchen. Shape your dough to create unique thumbprint charms, and combine with shop-bought beads to dangle from your ankle.

MATERIALS:

air-dry clay
small cookie cutter
straw
spray paint

leather cord
beads
craft glue
end caps and clasps

Tip: To make sure your thumbprints show up well, rub lotion or hand sanitizer over your thumb before making an imprint.

1. Pat or roll out the clay to about 0.3 centimetres (0.13 inch) thick.

2. Use the cookie cutter to cut out clay shapes. Use the straw to cut out a hole near the top of the shape.

3. Press your thumb firmly into the clay shape to make an indentation. You can make a single print, or layer two over each other to make a heart.

4. Air dry or bake clay according to package instructions. Let cool completely.

5. Set the shape on a protected work surface, and colour with spray paint. Let dry.

6. Cut a piece of the leather cord long enough to fit around your ankle plus 7.6 centimetres (3 inches). Fold the cord in half and thread through the hole in the charm. Decorate with beads.

7. Glue the ends of the cord and push them into the end caps. Let dry.

Heart wire and
CRYSTALS

*Give the special people in your life a homemade
heart they can keep close.*

MATERIALS:

wire cutter
24-gauge wire
round-nosed pliers
crystal beads
16-gauge wire

*Tip: Try bending shapes such as spirals,
triangles or ovals with your 24-gauge
wire. Or bend the wire into cursive words,
such as your name.*

1. Cut a 7.6-centimetre (3-inch) piece of the 24-gauge wire. Use the pliers to bend it into a heart shape.

2. String a bead onto the heart. Loop the ends of the wire to close the heart.

3. Cut one 20.3-centimetre (8-inch) piece of the 16-gauge wire. Bend one end around the heart's wire.

4. String beads onto the 16-guage wire, leaving a 0.6-centimetre (¼-inch) tail.

5. Close the 16-gauge wire around the other side of the heart.

Wire-wrapped
BEAD RING

Sometimes the prettiest accessories are the simplest.
With just three materials, you can make a
beautiful ring for a fun night out.

MATERIALS:
24-gauge wire
wire cutter
small beads

Tip: Put on as many beads as you want. You can even go all the way around the ring with beads. If you choose to do this, make sure the beads are small to prevent the ring from feeling too bulky.

1. Wrap wire loosely around your finger five times to size your ring. Cut.

2. Cut a 10.2-centimetre (4-inch) piece of wire. String three beads onto the wire, leaving a 0.6-centimetre (¼-inch) tail at the end. Line the beads up on top of the ring.

3. Wrap the smaller piece of wire around the ring several times to cover the tail. Continue wrapping the wire around the ring, weaving between the beads to hold them in place.

4. When most of the wire is wrapped, tuck the tail into a section of wrapped wire.

MATERIALS:
22-gauge wire
wire cutter
round-nosed pliers
small jump rings
seed beads
eye pins

Simply CHARMING

This tiny charm ring is another example of simple elegance. Wear several at a time for a statement piece that will draw the eye.

1. Wrap the wire around your finger and cut to desired length, plus 2.5 centimetres (1 inch).

2. Use the pliers to shape little loops at each end of the wire. Hook the loops together to close the ring.

3. Repeat steps 1 and 2 to create a second and third ring. Use a jump ring to attach the rings' loops, so instead of three small rings, you have one large one.

4. To make charms, thread one to three beads onto each eye pin. Bend a loop at the top and wrap the tail around the pin to keep the beads on the pin.

5. Repeat step 4 to create a second charm.

6. Attach the charms to the jump ring.

Tip: Small shop-bought charms also work well.

MATERIALS:

wool roving
foam pad and
   felting needle

needle and thread
small gems or beads

Wild and WOOLLY

Here's a fun way to introduce new materials into your accessory stash. Soft, wool fibre makes these rings comfortable to wear on fingers or toes.

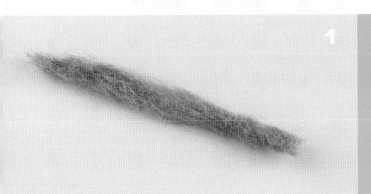

Tip: Sew just a few beads clustered together in one place, or space gems all around the outside of your ring.

1. Roll the wool roving between your fingers to create a tight, worm-shaped strand about 7.6 centimetres (3 inches) long.

2. Size the fibre around your finger, wrapping it around loosely a few times.

3. Continue to roll the looped fibre between your fingers until it stays together in a ring shape.

4. Place the fibre on the foam pad. Use the felting needle to poke the wool fibre multiple times until it holds together tightly.

5. Start sewing from the inside of your ring outwards, so the thread's knot is hidden. Sew tiny gems and beads to the outside of the ring.

Doughnut RING

Show off your tasteful fashion sense with a delicious doughnut ring.

MATERIALS:

light brown
   polymer clay
straw
pastel-coloured
   polymer clay

liquid polymer clay
toothpick
craft knife
metal glue
metal ring base

1. Knead the clay in your hands until soft. Roll light brown clay into small balls. Flatten slightly.

2. Use a straw to make a hole in the middle of the ball. Smooth out the hole to make a doughnut shape.

3. In a small bowl, combine very small pieces of pastel-coloured clay with a layer of liquid clay. Mix thoroughly until the pastel clay is liquefied.

4. Use a toothpick to dab the liquefied clay onto a doughnut to make icing.

5. Roll pieces of pastel clay so that they are very thin. Then cut tiny pieces with a craft knife to make sprinkles. You can also decorate your doughnuts with glitter or different colours of icing.

6. Bake doughnuts according to the instructions on the clay packet. Let cool completely before handling.

7. Use metal glue to attach a doughnut to a ring base. Let dry completely before wearing.

Tip: Lots of tiny food can be made from polymer clay! Ice cream cones, pretzels, cakes and fruit are only a few ideas. Make a cake or pizza, cut it into wedges and turn each wedge into a bracelet charm. Give a piece to each of your friends. It's the ultimate friendship bracelet!

Rock RING

This ring blends fashion with the natural world. Whether you use a polished stone or one just grabbed from the ground, you'll be sure to show off your outdoorsy side.

MATERIALS:

small rock
nail polish in
    several colours
clear nail polish

industrial-strength
    glue
metal ring base

Tip: Use sheer or natural-coloured polish for a subtle fashion statement. You can also use toothpicks or fine-tip brushes to add small details to your design.

1. Make sure the rock is completely clean by wiping off any dirt.

2. Use nail polish to paint a design on the rock, if desired. Let dry.

3. Apply a clear coat of nail polish to protect the coloured layers and add shine. Let dry.

4. Use industrial-strength glue to attach the rock to the ring base.

MATERIALS:

large button with two holes
smaller button with two holes
scissors
1.3-cm- (½-inch-) wide ribbon
paintbrush
fabric stiffener
clear nail polish
fabric glue

Button BLING

Looking forward to a fun get-together with the girls? Your blingy button bracelet will catch the eye of all your friends!

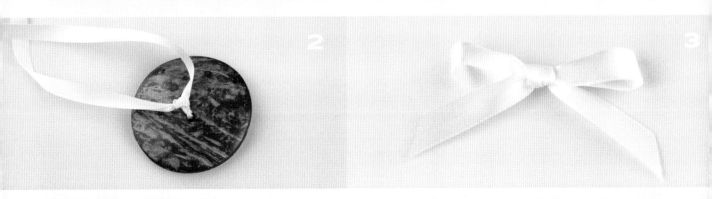

1. Stack the buttons on top of each other.

2. Cut a 12.7-centimetre (5-inch) piece of ribbon. Thread the ends down through the buttonholes. Use the ribbon to tie the buttons together.

3. Cut a 17.8-centimetre (7-inch) piece of ribbon. Tie the ribbon into a small bow and cut off the ends at an angle.

4. Paint a thin layer of fabric stiffener over the entire bow. Let dry.

5. Add a coat of clear nail polish to the bow. Let dry.

6. Glue the bow to the top of the button ring.

7. To wear, tie the ribbon around your wrist.

Tips: Make sure you buy buttons that have holes large enough to lace the ribbon.

To make a matching necklace, make a second bow and add jump rings to each side. Attach the jump rings to a thin chain.

Woven RING

Spice up your party attire with this simple, yet memorable design. The ring is smooth and flat, so it fits comfortably on your toe.

MATERIALS:

wire cutter
16-gauge wire
thin leather cord
fabric glue

Tip: If you don't have leather cord, you can weave other materials into your ring. Try making this ring with ribbon, wire or embroidery floss.

1. Cut a 17.8-centimetre (7-inch) piece of wire. Bend the wire around your toe three times. Trim off any extra wire.

2. Cut a 25.4-centimetre (10-inch) piece of leather cord.

3. Use the basket weave technique to weave the cord all the way around the ring.

4. Once you reach your starting point, cut off any extra cord.

5. Use the fabric glue to hold the two cord ends together. Let the glue dry completely before wearing your ring.

HOW TO BASKET WEAVE

Weave the leather cord over and under the three wire rings. Make sure the cord stays tight. Repeat, weaving back and forth, until the ring is covered. Then tuck in any loose ends.

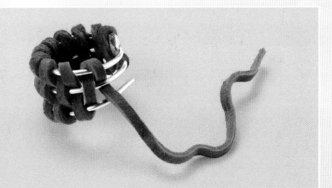

Toe ring and ANKLET

This design is a guaranteed attention grabber.
It features both an anklet and a toe ring – the perfect
way to accessorize your pedicure.

MATERIALS:

scissors
beading elastic
one large bead
seed beads
bead clamps
  with loops

round-nose pliers
20-gauge wire
wire cutter
clasp

1. Cut two 25.4-centimetre (10-inch) pieces of elastic.

2. String both pieces of elastic through the large bead, positioning the large bead in the middle.

3. To make your anklet, thread seed beads on both sides of one of the elastic strings. Leave a 1.3-centimetre (½-inch) tail at both ends.

4. Thread each tail through a bead clamp. Use pliers to secure the clamps. Trim away any extra elastic. Attach the clasp to the bead clamp loops.

5. Cut a 5-centimetre (2-inch) piece of the 20-gauge wire and shape and size around your toe. Use pliers to curl the wire ends into loops.

6. Thread seed beads on the second piece of elastic. Leave a 0.6-centimetre (¼-inch) tail at both ends. Thread the tails through the toe ring loops and secure with a bead clamp.

Tip: For extra flair, try a tiny tassel instead of a large bead.

Find out more

Button Jewellery, Marrianne Mercer (Search Press, 2011)

Compendium of Beading Techniques, Jean Power (Search Press, 2009)

Modern Friendship Bracelets, Pam Leach (Search Press, 2014)

About the author

Debbie Prestine Kachidurian has been a teacher and a writer for more than 20 years. She has taught in the primary school classroom, but especially enjoys creating and teaching enrichment classes such as wearable art, edible art and art history for kids. She enjoyed co-authoring this book with her daughters, Kelly and Megan.

Books in this series: